JOHN CENA

Wrestling Glory, Hollywood Stardom,
and Beyond

Steve Clowers

This book is a work of non-fiction and is based on the research and experiences of the author. While every effort has been made to ensure the accuracy and completeness of the information presented, the author and the publisher assume no responsibility for errors or omissions, or for damages resulting from the use of the information contained herein.

Content

Introduction

In the world of entertainment, there are few individuals who embody the essence of relentless determination and the indomitable "Never Give Up" spirit quite like John Cena. His multifaceted career has taken him on an extraordinary journey, from the electrifying confines of the professional wrestling ring to the dazzling lights of Hollywood. As we embark on this exploration of his remarkable life and career, we'll uncover the threads of his early aspirations, his meteoric rise in the world of professional wrestling, and his seamless transition into a Hollywood heavyweight, all while witnessing the unwavering flame of his "Never Give Up" ethos.

John Cena's life story is a testament to the power of unyielding dedication and a passion for captivating audiences worldwide. It's a tale that transcends mere entertainment, weaving together chapters of triumph, charisma, and, above all, the unwavering commitment to never surrender in the face of adversity. His is a story of a man who not only speaks the words "Never Give Up" but lives and breathes them, inspiring countless individuals along the way.

From the pulse-pounding excitement of WWE events to the silver screen's glitz and glamour, John Cena's journey is an awe-inspiring reminder that dreams can be achieved through sheer willpower and the refusal to back down. As we delve into the highs, the lows, and the incredible spirit of a man who has redefined what it means to be a wrestling legend, an actor, and a cultural icon, we'll witness firsthand the force that is John Cena.

Welcome to the captivating world of a true champion – both in the ring and in life. Welcome to Exploring the Phenomenal Career of WWE Icon John Cena, from the Ring to the Silver Screen, with a Glimpse into His Impact on Pop Culture.

Chapter 1

Who is JOHN CENA?

His Early Life

The early years of John Cena's life set the stage for his remarkable journey as a global icon. Born on April 23, 1977, in West Newbury, Massachusetts, John Felix Anthony Cena Jr. was raised in a close-knit family that emphasized the values of hard work and perseverance.

From a young age, Cena displayed a strong passion for sports, particularly football and bodybuilding. He attended Cushing

Academy, where his athletic talents shone, especially in football. These early athletic pursuits hinted at the unwavering determination that would define his future career.

After high school, Cena pursued higher education at Springfield College in Massachusetts, where he continued to excel in football. However, his academic pursuits were just the beginning of his journey. It was during these formative years that he discovered a profound love for professional wrestling, a passion that would shape his destiny.

John Cena's early life not only laid the groundwork for his athletic achievements but also offered a glimpse into his unyielding spirit. This spirit, evident even in his youth, foreshadowed the mantra that would become his trademark throughout his career: "Never Give Up." As we delve further into his story, we will explore how this spirit propelled him into the world of professional wrestling and beyond, ultimately leaving an enduring impact on fans worldwide.

His Background

John Cena's background is a fascinating blend of family values, athletic pursuits, and an enduring spirit. He was born in West Newbury, Massachusetts, to parents Carol and John Felix Anthony Cena Sr. John's family has always been at the heart of his life, and he shares this journey with four brothers: Dan, Matt, Steve, and Sean. John occupies the second eldest position in this closely-knit family, forging deep bonds that have sustained him throughout his life.

His early years were marked by a strong focus on academics and a profound love for sports, particularly football. John Cena's talents shone brightly during his time at Cushing Academy, where he excelled not only in the classroom but also on the football field. This period of his life laid the groundwork for his future success.

As he continued his education at Springfield College in Massachusetts, Cena's passion for both academics and sports persisted. It was during these formative years that he discovered a new calling – professional wrestling. This discovery would go on to shape the course of his life, propelling him into a world of entertainment and athleticism that few could have predicted.

Yet, beyond the athletic and academic achievements, John Cena's background is deeply rooted in the "Never Give Up" ethos. This principle, instilled in him by his family and his own indomitable spirit, has been a guiding force throughout his career. It's a philosophy that has seen him through the highs and lows, both inside the wrestling ring and in the broader landscape of life.

Within this intricate mosaic of experiences and familial connections lies the compelling story of John Cena's transformation from a young dreamer to a global superstar, accomplished actor, and committed philanthropist. His family, comprising his parents and brothers, occupies a central place in this remarkable narrative, offering unwavering support and a strong foundation for his extraordinary journey.

Chapter 2

Wrestling Beginnings

John Cena's journey into the world of professional wrestling is a story deeply rooted in the influences of his childhood and the aspirations that ignited within him. Born and raised in West Newbury, Massachusetts, Cena's early years were marked by the presence of a family that cherished the excitement and spectacle of wrestling. His father, John Felix Anthony Cena Sr., was a fervent wrestling enthusiast who eagerly shared his passion with young John. This early exposure to the world of wrestling left an indelible impression on Cena, sparking the flames of ambition that would ultimately shape his career.

As a child, Cena found himself captivated by the larger-than-life personas and electrifying performances of wrestling legends like Hulk Hogan, The Rock, and Stone Cold Steve Austin. Their charisma, athleticism, and ability to command the audience's attention resonated deeply with him. Cena's admiration for these iconic figures fueled his own dreams of one day stepping into the squared circle, where he could captivate audiences and etch his name into wrestling history.

The world of professional wrestling became more than just a form of entertainment for young John; it became a dream, a calling that he felt destined to pursue. These early experiences and influences laid the foundation for the passion that would drive him to the pinnacle of wrestling success.

Professional Wrestling Journey: Training and Breakthrough

John Cena's path to professional wrestling stardom was far from a smooth and effortless ascent. It was a journey marked by rigorous training, unwavering dedication, and a relentless pursuit of his dreams. After completing his education at Springfield College in Massachusetts, Cena took a significant step towards realizing his wrestling aspirations by enrolling in the Ultimate Pro Wrestling (UPW) School in California.

Under the tutelage of seasoned trainers, Cena embarked on a transformative period of learning and growth. He honed his wrestling skills, developed his unique charisma, and refined the art of storytelling within the ring. It was during this time that he began to carve out the persona that would later make him a household name in the wrestling world.

In 2002, John Cena's tireless efforts bore fruit when he inked a contract with WWE (World Wrestling Entertainment). This pivotal moment marked the official commencement of his professional wrestling journey on the grandest stage of them all. Cena made his debut on the main WWE roster, an entry into a world of fierce competition, larger-than-life personalities, and adoring fans.

Cena's early wrestling persona was characterized by a brash, freestyle-rapping, and ruthless competitor. His quick-witted banter and unyielding determination quickly set him apart from the pack, earning him a rapidly growing fan base. In 2004, he achieved a major milestone by capturing the United States Championship, solidifying his status as a rising star in WWE.

This breakthrough was just the beginning of what would become a remarkable ascent to the upper echelons of professional wrestling. Cena's journey exemplifies the age-old adage that success is not achieved overnight; it's the product of unrelenting commitment, tireless effort, and a never-ending pursuit of excellence.

Championship Accomplishments and Rise to Prominence

John Cena's journey through the WWE was marked by a series of significant milestones and championship triumphs that solidified his status as a wrestling superstar. After capturing the United States Championship, Cena's ascent within the organization continued with remarkable momentum.

In 2005, he achieved one of the most coveted accomplishments in WWE by winning the WWE Championship at WrestleMania 21. This victory catapulted him into the upper echelons of the wrestling world, marking the beginning of an era often referred to as the "Cena Era." His reign as WWE Champion was characterized by intense rivalries, epic battles, and a growing legion of fans known as the "Cenation."

Cena's charismatic persona, never-give-up attitude, and resilience in the face of adversity resonated deeply with fans of all ages. He became a symbol of hope and inspiration, both inside and outside the wrestling ring. Cena's championship accomplishments continued to stack up, with multiple WWE Championship reigns and reigns as World Heavyweight Champion.

His feuds with some of the greatest names in professional wrestling, including the likes of The Rock, Randy Orton, and Edge, became legendary. These rivalries not only showcased Cena's in-ring abilities but also his ability to connect with audiences on an emotional level. Whether he was the hero or the anti-hero, Cena's character evolved, adapting to the ever-changing dynamics of WWE storytelling.

Catchphrases and Signature Moves

A defining aspect of John Cena's wrestling persona was the creation of memorable catchphrases and signature moves that became synonymous with his name. Perhaps the most iconic catchphrase was "Never Give Up," a motto that encapsulated his resilience and determination. The sight of Cena rising from seemingly insurmountable odds, fueled by the rallying cry of "Never Give Up," became a hallmark of his matches.

Another catchphrase that resonated with fans was "The Champ is Here!" It signaled his arrival and dominance in the wrestling world, often followed by a passionate and energetic response from the audience.

In addition to catchphrases, Cena possessed a repertoire of signature moves that thrilled fans. The "Attitude Adjustment" (formerly known as the "F-U") and the "STF" (Stepover Toehold Facelock) were his primary finishing maneuvers, both capable of securing him victories in high-stakes matches.

John Cena's ability to engage the crowd, tell compelling stories in the ring, and deliver electrifying moments solidified his place as one of the most iconic wrestlers in WWE history. His impact extended far beyond the wrestling ring, transcending into the realms of entertainment, philanthropy, and pop culture.

Chapter 3

WWE Career

John Cena's WWE career is nothing short of legendary, marked by a slew of achievements and records that firmly established him as one of the most celebrated WWE superstars of all time.

Cena's list of accomplishments is extensive. He is a record-holder for the most WWE World Heavyweight Championship reigns, an honor that reflects his dominance and longevity within the wrestling world. Cena's championship reigns were not just about winning titles but also about defending them with unwavering determination, showcasing his resilience.

His accolades include multiple victories in marquee events like WrestleMania, where he faced off against some of the biggest names in the business. His memorable clashes with legends such as The Rock and his rivalry with Randy Orton are etched in WWE history.

Beyond championship reigns, John Cena was a pioneer in various match types, from the innovative "Elimination Chamber" to the grueling "I Quit" match. His willingness to push the boundaries of entertainment and athleticism added depth to his character and provided fans with unforgettable moments.

Signature Moves and Iconic Catchphrases

What set John Cena apart in the wrestling world were not just his victories but also the memorable moments he created through signature moves and iconic catchphrases.

The "Attitude Adjustment" (formerly known as the "F-U") became a defining move in Cena's arsenal. It involved hoisting opponents onto his shoulders and slamming them down to the canvas, often signaling the beginning of the end for his opponents. This move showcased his incredible strength and agility, and fans eagerly anticipated its execution.

Another signature move, the "STF" (Stepover Toehold Facelock), was Cena's submission hold. When locked in, it signaled that his opponent was in a world of pain, with Cena's unwavering resolve to secure victory on full display.

Cena's catchphrases were equally iconic. "Never Give Up" wasn't just a motto; it was a rallying cry that resonated with fans and symbolized his resilience in the face of adversity. "The Champ is Here!" was a proclamation that heralded his arrival and domination, igniting the crowd with energy.

These catchphrases and signature moves weren't just tools of the trade; they were expressions of Cena's character and values. They embodied his never-give-up spirit, his dedication to entertaining the WWE

Universe, and his commitment to leaving an indelible mark on the wrestling landscape.

John Cena's WWE career represents a journey of remarkable achievements, resilience, and an unwavering connection with fans. His legacy continues to inspire aspiring wrestlers and entertain millions worldwide, making him a true icon in the annals of professional wrestling history.

Chapter 4

Transition to Acting

John Cena's journey from the world of professional wrestling to the glitzy realm of Hollywood has been nothing short of remarkable. This transition, which began as a daring leap of faith, has seen Cena evolve from a WWE superstar into a respected actor with a burgeoning filmography and a promising future in the entertainment industry. In this exploration, we will delve into the compelling narrative of Cena's transition to acting, his early roles, notable filmography, and the impact he's had on the silver screen.

The Genesis of Transition

For John Cena, the transition to acting was not an overnight phenomenon but rather a deliberate and calculated move. As he reached the zenith of his wrestling career, Cena began contemplating the next chapter of his life. It was a juncture where he looked beyond the confines of the wrestling ring, seeking fresh challenges and opportunities to showcase his talent.

Cena's charisma and on-screen presence in WWE had already demonstrated his ability to captivate audiences. He possessed a unique blend of charm, humor, and authenticity that transcended wrestling and held the potential to resonate in other forms of entertainment, particularly in the realm of acting.

The turning point arrived with his cameo appearance in the 2006 action film "The Marine." While the film received mixed critical reviews, Cena's performance was noted for its energy and potential. This opportunity, though modest in scale, offered Cena a glimpse into the world of filmmaking and ignited a spark that would eventually lead him down the path to acting.

Early Roles and Learning the Craft

Following "The Marine," Cena's foray into acting was marked by a series of roles in films such as "12 Rounds" and "Legendary." These early films provided Cena with the chance to hone his acting skills and gain valuable experience in front of the camera.

While critical acclaim may have been limited during this phase, Cena's commitment to improving as an actor was evident. He was dedicated to learning the craft and proving that his talents extended beyond the wrestling ring. This period of adjustment allowed him to understand the nuances of acting, adapt to different genres, and collaborate with seasoned actors and directors.

Cena's journey was not without its challenges. Transitioning from a high-octane, physically demanding profession like professional wrestling to the subtleties of acting required a significant shift in approach. It demanded a willingness to embrace vulnerability, immerse himself in character development, and explore the depths of emotion that acting demands.

Notable Filmography

As Cena continued to develop his acting prowess, his filmography began to expand. One of his breakthrough moments came with his role as Agent Ford Brody in the 2015 film "Trainwreck," directed by Judd Apatow and starring Amy Schumer. Cena's portrayal of a sensitive but comedic character garnered attention and signaled his potential as a versatile actor.

In 2017, Cena made his mark in the blockbuster franchise "The Fast and the Furious," joining the ensemble cast of

"The Fate of the Furious." His character, the charismatic and resourceful government agent Luke Hobbs, resonated with audiences and added a new dimension to the film series. Cena's charisma and chemistry with co-stars like Dwayne "The Rock" Johnson elevated his status in the world of action cinema.

Cena's involvement in the "Fast & Furious" franchise continued with "F9: The Fast Saga," released in 2021. In this film, he reprised his role as Jakob Toretto, the estranged brother of Vin Diesel's character, Dominic Toretto. Cena's performance in this high-octane blockbuster showcased his action-hero capabilities and solidified his place in the franchise's evolving narrative.

Beyond action films, Cena has ventured into comedy with projects like "Blockers," where he played an overprotective father trying to prevent his daughter from losing her virginity on prom night. His comedic timing and willingness to tackle unconventional roles endeared him to both audiences and critics.

The Impact on Pop Culture

John Cena's transition to acting has not only reshaped his own career but has also left an indelible impact on pop culture.

He represents a shift in perception, proving that wrestlers can successfully cross over into mainstream acting, challenging stereotypes along the way.

His presence in Hollywood has introduced a new generation to his charisma and magnetism. He's become a sought-after talent, a recognizable face in both action-packed blockbusters and light-hearted comedies. Cena's contributions to film have expanded the reach of WWE and brought its brand to a wider audience.

Moreover, Cena's off-screen persona as a kind-hearted and philanthropic individual has further endeared him to fans and helped cement his status as a role model. He's utilized his fame to make a difference, engaging in numerous charitable initiatives and raising awareness for important causes.

Future Prospects and Beyond

As John Cena continues his journey in acting, his future prospects in the entertainment industry appear promising. He's set to star in various upcoming projects, including the superhero film "The Suicide Squad," where he portrays the character Peacemaker, and a spin-off series titled "Peacemaker," demonstrating his versatility in different media formats.

Cena's commitment to his craft, coupled with his relentless work ethic, suggests that his evolution as an actor is far from complete. He remains dedicated to pushing boundaries, embracing challenging roles, and expanding his artistic horizons.

John Cena's transition to acting represents a remarkable evolution in his career. It's a journey marked by determination, adaptability, and a willingness to take risks. From his humble beginnings as a WWE superstar to his current status as a Hollywood actor, Cena's story serves as an inspiration to those who dare to chase their dreams and prove that reinvention is possible, no matter where your journey begins.

Chapter 5

Television Hosting

John Cena's dynamic career extends beyond the wrestling ring and the silver screen; it includes a notable foray into television hosting. This multifaceted entertainer has ventured into the realm of television with charisma, enthusiasm, and a passion for connecting with audiences in diverse ways. In this exploration, we'll delve into Cena's journey as a television host, his notable hosting gigs, and the impact he's had in this vibrant and competitive entertainment landscape.

The Transition to Television Hosting

Cena's journey into television hosting was a natural extension of his career evolution. His years as a WWE superstar had already showcased his captivating presence, exceptional communication skills, and the ability to engage live audiences. These qualities served as the foundation upon which his television hosting career would be built.

One of Cena's earliest television hosting roles came with the reality competition show "Are You Smarter Than a 5th Grader?" in 2018. This opportunity marked his debut as a television host and offered a glimpse into his ability to navigate the hosting landscape. Cena's down-to-earth demeanor, relatable personality, and knack for humor endeared him to contestants and viewers alike.

"WWE SmackDown Live" Hosting

Cena's connection to WWE remained strong even as he ventured into other areas of entertainment. In 2016, he returned to WWE's weekly programming, "SmackDown Live," as a part-time performer. In addition to his in-ring appearances, Cena also took on hosting duties for the show on several occasions.

As a host, Cena skillfully bridged the gap between the wrestling action and the audience. He provided insightful commentary, conducted engaging interviews with WWE superstars, and added an extra layer of entertainment to the already exhilarating show. His presence in the hosting role was a testament to his versatility within the WWE brand.

"Are You Smarter Than a 5th Grader?"

One of Cena's most prominent television hosting roles came with the revival of "Are You Smarter Than a 5th Grader?" in 2019. This family-friendly game show, originally created by Mark Burnett, tested contestants' knowledge against questions typically found in elementary school textbooks.

As the host of the show, Cena embraced the role with enthusiasm and charm. His interactions with the contestants, who ranged from adults to children, showcased his ability to connect with people from all walks of life. Cena's humor and lighthearted approach added a layer of entertainment to the educational premise of the show.

"Are You Smarter Than a 5th Grader?" was a platform for Cena to not only display his hosting talents but also to demonstrate his commitment to education. His passion for learning and dedication to charitable causes aligned seamlessly with the show's educational theme.

"Wipeout" Hosting

Cena's hosting journey continued to flourish when he took the reins of the iconic obstacle course competition series, "Wipeout," in 2021. As the host, Cena guided contestants through an array of hilariously challenging obstacles while providing comedic commentary and witty banter.

His role as the host of "Wipeout" showcased Cena's versatility as an entertainer. He brought an energetic and charismatic presence to the show, creating an engaging and entertaining experience for viewers of all ages. Cena's ability to connect with contestants and viewers added a fresh and dynamic dimension to the show's reboot.

Cena's Impact on Television Hosting

John Cena's impact as a television host extends beyond the screen. His hosting roles have demonstrated his versatility as an entertainer, showcasing his ability to seamlessly transition between the worlds of wrestling, acting, and television.

Cena's hosting gigs have also highlighted his genuine and relatable personality. He approaches his hosting duties with a sense of authenticity, making contestants and audiences alike feel comfortable and engaged. This authenticity, coupled with his charismatic demeanor, has endeared him to fans and elevated the quality of the shows he hosts.

Furthermore, Cena's commitment to charitable endeavors has remained a consistent theme throughout his television hosting career. His involvement in educational initiatives and his support for various charitable causes align with the positive and uplifting spirit of the shows he hosts.

As John Cena's television hosting career continues to evolve, there's a sense of anticipation regarding the future projects he will undertake. His ability to connect with diverse audiences and his natural charisma make him a sought-after host for a wide range of television formats, from game shows to reality competitions and beyond.

Cena's journey as a television host exemplifies his dedication to diversifying his entertainment portfolio while maintaining the qualities that have made him a beloved figure in the world of entertainment. His hosting roles add yet another layer to his multifaceted career, solidifying his place as an enduring and influential presence in the entertainment industry.

John Cena's television hosting journey is a testament to his versatility as an entertainer and his ability to captivate audiences in diverse mediums. From game shows to reality competitions, his hosting roles showcase his charisma, authenticity, and commitment to entertaining and inspiring viewers. As Cena continues to make his mark in the world of television hosting, audiences can look forward to more memorable moments and engaging entertainment from this charismatic and multifaceted entertainer.

Chapter 6

John Cena Personal Life beyond the spot light

John Cena's life in the public eye is often characterized by his wrestling career, acting endeavors, and television hosting roles. However, his personal life paints a portrait of a man whose journey is defined by values, passions, relationships, and a commitment to making a positive impact. In this expansive exploration, we'll delve into John Cena's personal life, covering his early years, family, relationships, and the principles that have guided him both in and out of the spotlight.

John Cena was raised in a close-knit family in West Newbury, Massachusetts. His parents, Carol and John Cena Sr., instilled in him the values of hard work, perseverance, and the importance of family bonds. Cena shared his upbringing with four brothers: Dan, Matt, Steve, and Sean. As the second eldest among his siblings, Cena developed a strong sense of camaraderie and support within his family unit.

Cena's early years were marked by a blend of academic pursuits and a deep passion for sports. He excelled in football during his time at Cushing Academy and continued to showcase his athletic prowess at Springfield College in

Massachusetts. It was during these formative years that he discovered his profound love for professional wrestling, a passion that would eventually become a defining element of his life.

The "Never Give Up" Spirit

A fundamental aspect of John Cena's personal life is his unwavering commitment to the philosophy of "Never Give Up." This ethos, which became a hallmark of his wrestling persona, was deeply ingrained in his upbringing. Cena's family, particularly his father, played a significant role in nurturing this spirit of determination and resilience.

This "Never Give Up" attitude has been a guiding force throughout Cena's life and career. It has propelled him through the challenges and triumphs of his wrestling journey, serving as a source of inspiration for millions of fans around the world. Beyond wrestling, Cena has applied this philosophy to various aspects of his life, from his acting career to his endeavors in other entertainment fields.

Relationships and Personal Growth

John Cena's personal life has been marked by significant relationships that have contributed to his growth and evolution as an individual. His marriage to Elizabeth Huberdeau was a notable chapter in his life, but the couple later divorced.

Cena's high-profile relationship with fellow WWE superstar Nikki Bella garnered significant media attention. The couple became a central focus of the reality TV series "Total Divas" and its spin-off "Total Bellas." Their engagement at WrestleMania 33 was a moment of public celebration, but ultimately, the engagement was called off. Cena's candidness about the complexities of relationships and his willingness to address these challenges in public discussions have resonated with many.

In 2020, Cena surprised fans by quietly marrying Shay Shariatzadeh, a Canadian engineer, in a private ceremony. This low-key approach to their relationship reflected Cena's desire to maintain a degree of privacy while embracing this new chapter of his personal life.

Fitness and Wellness

Fitness has been a consistent theme in John Cena's personal life. His dedication to physical fitness has been an integral part of his persona, both in WWE and in the world of entertainment. Cena's workouts are legendary, reflecting his discipline and commitment to maintaining peak physical condition.

His passion for fitness extends beyond aesthetics; it aligns with his advocacy for a healthy lifestyle. Cena has authored books on fitness and nutrition, offering guidance to those looking to improve their well-being. His commitment to wellness serves as an inspiration to many, reinforcing the idea that physical health is a crucial component of personal growth.

Privacy and Balance

Despite his fame and public persona, John Cena values his privacy and strives to strike a balance between his personal and public life. This balance has become increasingly important as he navigates a career that spans wrestling, acting, television hosting, and various entertainment fields.

Cena's ability to maintain a level of privacy while remaining accessible to fans is a testament to his skill in controlling the narrative of his life. He shares aspects of his personal journey selectively, offering fans a glimpse into his world while safeguarding what matters most to him.

Future Prospects and Legacy

As John Cena's career continues to evolve, his personal life remains a source of inspiration for those who admire his determination, resilience, and commitment to living life on his terms. His journey reflects the principles of hard work, family values, and a "Never Give Up" attitude that have guided him both in and out of the spotlight, leaving a lasting legacy in the world of entertainment.

Chapter 7

Legacy and Impact

John Cena's legacy in the world of professional wrestling, entertainment, and beyond is indelible. Throughout his career, he has left an enduring impact that stretches far beyond the confines of the wrestling ring. In this exploration of his legacy and impact, we'll delve into the lasting contributions and influence of this multifaceted entertainer.

Influence in Professional Wrestling

John Cena's influence in professional wrestling is immeasurable. He emerged as a torchbearer of the WWE during the 2000s and became the face of the company. His charismatic persona, incredible work ethic, and unwavering commitment to entertaining fans elevated WWE's status on a global scale.

Cena's "Never Give Up" spirit resonated with audiences of all ages. He became a role model to young fans, embodying qualities of determination, perseverance, and resilience. His memorable catchphrases and signature moves, such as the "Attitude Adjustment" and "STF," became synonymous with his name and left an indelible mark on wrestling history.

His championship reigns, including a record-breaking 16 WWE World Championship victories, solidified his status as one of the all-time greats. Cena's rivalries with legends like The Rock, Randy Orton, and Edge added to his storied career, creating unforgettable moments and matches.

Transition to Hollywood

John Cena's transition to Hollywood marked a significant shift in his career, and his impact in the world of acting continues to grow. He shattered stereotypes about wrestlers crossing over into mainstream entertainment, proving that his talents extended far beyond the wrestling ring.

His roles in blockbuster franchises like "The Fast and the Furious" showcased his versatility as an actor and introduced him to a global audience. Cena's charisma and ability to connect with viewers translated seamlessly to the silver screen, solidifying his place as a sought-after talent.

Cena's television hosting roles, whether in game shows like "Are You Smarter Than a 5th Grader?" or hosting WWE's

"SmackDown Live," demonstrated his ability to engage and entertain diverse audiences. His charisma and authenticity as a host added value to various television programs and endeared him to fans.

Positive Impact and Philanthropy

Beyond the spotlight, John Cena's impact is exemplified by his philanthropic efforts and commitment to making a difference. He leveraged his fame to support causes close to his heart, granting hundreds of wishes for children through the Make-A-Wish Foundation. His charitable endeavors extended to causes such as breast cancer awareness and support for military veterans.

Cena's "Never Give Up" mentality transcended wrestling and became a source of inspiration to those facing adversity. His willingness to address personal challenges, such as relationships and public scrutiny, demonstrated vulnerability and resonated with many, encouraging open conversations about mental health.

John Cena's legacy extends beyond his accomplishments in wrestling, acting, and hosting. He leaves a legacy of inspiration, showing that dedication, hard work, and authenticity can lead to extraordinary success. His ability to connect with people from all walks of life, from young wrestling fans to moviegoers, speaks to his universal appeal.

Cena's legacy is a testament to his impact on the entertainment industry and his unwavering commitment to leaving a positive imprint on the world. As he continues to evolve and take on new challenges, his legacy remains a source of inspiration for those who believe in the power of resilience, authenticity, and the spirit of "Never Give Up."

The conclusion

In the annals of entertainment and sports, few figures have shone as brightly and transcended as many boundaries as John Cena. His journey from the squared circle of professional wrestling to the silver screen, television hosting, and philanthropy has been nothing short of remarkable. As we reflect on his enduring legacy and look forward to his future ventures, one thing becomes abundantly clear: John Cena is a force of nature, an icon whose impact knows no bounds.

Cena's ability to capture the hearts and imaginations of fans, whether in the electric atmosphere of WWE arenas or on the grand stages of Hollywood, is a testament to his universal appeal. His charisma, authenticity, and undeniable talent have made him a beloved figure whose influence stretches far beyond the realms of wrestling and entertainment.

As he continues his journey, Cena's ongoing pursuits promise even more exciting chapters in an already storied career. His dedication to acting, television hosting, and philanthropy remains unwavering. With each new role, project, or philanthropic initiative, Cena reaffirms his commitment to excellence and his desire to leave a lasting impact on the world.

In the world of acting, Cena's star continues to rise, and his roles in blockbuster films are a testament to his versatility as an actor. He's poised to take on new challenges, explore different genres, and captivate audiences with his talent. With each role, he adds depth to his already impressive filmography, leaving an indelible mark on the silver screen.

As a television host, Cena's ability to engage and entertain audiences across various formats showcases his versatility and relatability. His future in television is bright, offering countless opportunities to connect with viewers and create memorable moments.

Cena's philanthropic efforts, while not mentioned in this conclusion, will undoubtedly continue to make a profound difference in the lives of those in need. His compassion and dedication to giving back serve as an enduring source of inspiration.

John Cena's journey is a testament to the power of passion, resilience, and unwavering commitment. His ongoing pursuits and future ventures promise to be as captivating and impactful as the chapters that have come before.

Cena's legacy is a living testament to the idea that with talent, hard work, and a relentless pursuit of one's dreams, the possibilities are endless. As we eagerly anticipate what lies ahead for this iconic entertainer, one thing remains certain: the future is brighter with John Cena in it.

Made in the USA
Columbia, SC
17 November 2024

f6faedf3-e845-42c2-b99a-94b3bfaab8b0R01